How I Learned to Make Friends

by Amy Z. Rowland

The Center for Applied Psychology, Inc.
King of Prussia, PA

How I Learned to Make Friends

By Amy Z. Rowland
Illustrated by Jille Mandel
Designed by Charles Brenna

Other books in the "How To" Series...
• How I Learned To Control My Temper
• How I Learned To Be Considerate
• How I Learned To Think Things Through

Published by:
The Center for Applied Psychology, Inc.
P.O. Box 61587, King of Prussia, PA 19406 U.S.A.
Tel. 1-800-962-1141

The Center for Applied Psychology, Inc. is the publisher of Childswork/Childsplay, a catalog of products for mental health professionals, teachers, and parents who wish to help children with their social and emotional growth.

Second Printing

ISBN: 1-882732-29-4

INTRODUCTION

HOW I LEARNED TO MAKE FRIENDS is a storybook and workbook in one. The first half of the book is a story about Alicia, who has a hard time making friends. Alicia learns a variety of ways to be a friend and to have friends. She learns she is treated better by other children when she talks things out rather than acting them out.

The second half of the book teaches readers the same by completing 30 activities aimed at helping kids understand how to make friends and keep them. These reproducible and fun exercises teach children how to identify the differences in people, how to recognize what others are feeling, how to make friends, and much more!

A lot of stories begin 'Once upon a time," so I think I'll start that way, too. But my 'once upon a time' wasn't a long time ago. It was at the beginning of this year.

Once upon a time, I was invited to a birthday party
at Cindy's house . . .

Mom wrapped up the doll with pretty paper and ribbons.

On Saturday, after Cindy blew out the candles on her cake,
I gave her my present.

Cindy tore off the paper and ribbons and opened up the
package. She took out the doll.

Then she put the doll down on top of all her other presents.

Cindy was still opening presents, but I took the doll and I held it. I always wanted a doll like that.

I ran all the way home.

I was so sad I couldn't stop thinking about it.

When my mother saw me with the doll, she frowned.
She knew something was very wrong.
I went to my room and I shut my door. I looked at the doll.

Then, mom came to the door.

24

So I told my mom that Cindy didn't want to play with the doll that I got her, and that was rude of her, and everyone got mad at me, and then I took the doll back and went home.

I got sadder and sadder.
I thought, maybe I won't ever have any friends again.

So I asked my mother how to make friends.

I said,"Uncle George knows how to be a friend. I can talk to him about my problems. He really listens. And if I'm not ready to talk, he says, 'that's OK.' He never tells me what to do. He always asks, 'Alicia, what do you think you should do?'"

"She does," I said. "So does Stewart."

"Stewart shares. He shares his sandwiches at lunch when kids forget their lunch boxes. He even shares his best toys with everyone when we play after school."

On the next Monday, I brought the doll in to school. I gave it to
Cindy at recess. I said, "I'm sorry I upset you at your
birthday party. I really want you to have the doll."

I didn't know what she would say.

Then she smiled. "Thank you for the doll, Alicia," Cindy said. "I still had a nice birthday party. We're still friends."

That day after school, Cindy, Sarah, Julie and I all walked home together. It's so great to have friends!

I love playing with my friends.

I feel good when I help my friends.

Friends are great when you have things in common.

There are so many ways to be friends.

That day was such an important day, I wrote
about it in my diary. I wrote, "Today I learned
how to make friends. This is how I do it."

1. I smile at people and try to be nice to be around.

2. I let people know that I care about how they are feeling.

3. I listen when my friends need someone to talk to.

4. I understand when my friends don't want to talk, or even be with me all the time.

5. I don't tell my friends what to do. I _ask_ what they want to do and sometimes do things with them.

6. When I have something to say, I say it in a kind way.

7. I know when to say I'm sorry.

8. I share with the people I care about.

9. I am thankful for my friends.

10. I treat everyone the way I want to be treated.

That's my story. The end.

How i Learned to Make Friends

Activity Book

1. Friendly People

Mom asked me to think about all the people I know who are friendly to me. I thought of Uncle George and Carla and Stewart. This is what I wrote down:

Uncle George – Always listens when I need to talk.

Carla – Always asks me how I am doing today.

Stewart – Shares his lunch with me sometimes.

Who are the friendly people that you know? Make a list of their names and why you think they are friendly.

FRIENDLY PEOPLE   HOW THEY ARE FRIENDLY

_____   _____

_____   _____

_____   _____

_____   _____

_____   _____

_____   _____

2. Who Are My Friends?

I'm going to make a scrapbook with pictures in it of my friends. You can make a scrapbook, too. Ask each of your friends for a picture. Paste the picture in the square and write the name of your friend underneath.

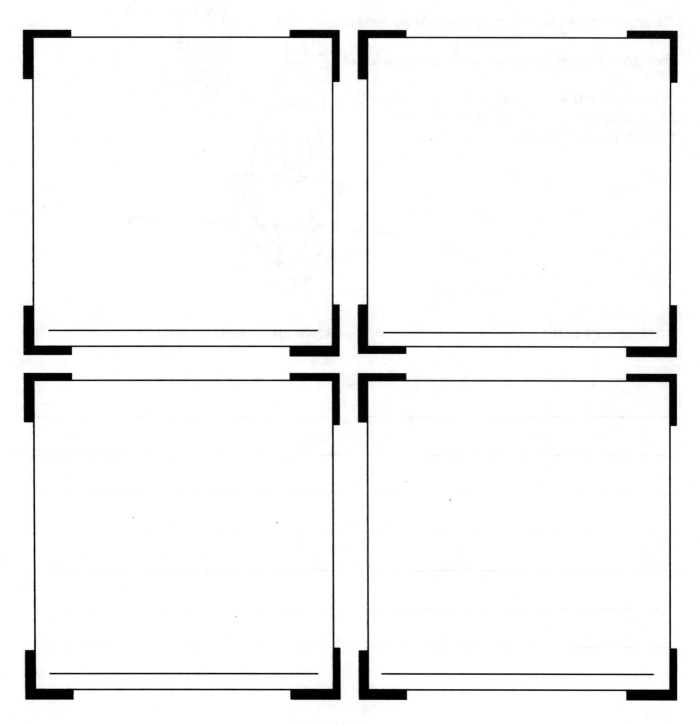

3. Best Friend

My best friend is Cindy, because when we walk home from school together, we can talk about anything. I know she really cares about me. When I missed school two weeks ago, she called me at home to give me my homework assignments. I really like Cindy.

Who is your best friend? Draw his or her picture. Write her name underneath the picture. Talk about how she has been a good friend to you.

4. Discovering Things You Have in Common

• •

Cindy and I walk home from school together the same way. Jason and I practice soccer together on Saturdays because we both like to kick the ball around. Sharing experiences is called having things in common.

What do you have in common with your friends? Cut out pictures from magazines that show activities you do with your friends. Paste the pictures in the boxes. Write a sentence about each friend and what you have in common, like this: "Jason and I practice soccer." If you need help, ask for it from a grown-up.

Jason and I
practice soccer.

5. Appreciating Differences

My friend Suzie Chang is very different from me. She looks different. She talks differently.
She lives in a house very different from mine. I have learned many things from her that
make me like having friends who are different from me. I even learned how to eat Chinese
food with chopsticks!

Who are your friends who are different? What have you learned from these differences?
Draw them in the boxes below.

Suzie showed me
how to use chop-
sticks.

6. Wish Book

Who would you like to have as a friend? Draw this person's picture. Write his or her name underneath. What could you do that might help you to become friends with this person?

7. Understanding Feelings

To be a friend, you must consider your friend's feelings as much as your own. Looking at the way your friends stand or sit can tell you a lot about how they are feeling. Look at these pictures of my friends. How do you think Cindy, Sarah, and Julie feel?

How does Cindy feel? What makes people feel that way?

_____

_____

_____

_____

How does Sarah feel? What makes people feel that way?

_____

_____

_____

_____

How does Julie feel? What makes people feel that way?

_____

_____

_____

_____

8. Facial Expressions

Looking at your friend's face can tell you a lot about how your friend is feeling. Look at the faces of these kids in my class at school. Can you help me decide how they are feeling? I really want to know.

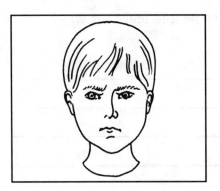

What is Bobby feeling? What makes people feel this way?

_____

_____

_____

What is Suzie feeling? What makes people feel this way?

_____

_____

_____

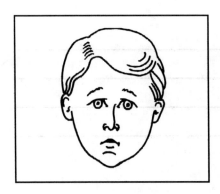

What is George feeling? What makes people feel this way?

_____

_____

_____

9. Mixed Messages

I've noticed that sometimes what my friend says and what my friend does don't always match. Sometimes I ask Julie if she's okay, and she says, "Sure, I'm okay," but she looks like something is really bothering her. Has this ever happened to you?

Look at the pictures of these kids in my class. Beside each picture, I've written down what they *said* they were feeling. Draw a line from the picture to the words that best describe the feeling in the picture. That would help me out a lot.

"This is fun."

"I feel okay."

"I know what I'm doing."

"I don't feel so good."

10. Showing You Care

Carla is really good at talking to people in a way that shows she cares about what they are feeling. She asks caring questions a lot. Here are some I've heard her ask. Can you think of any others?

"Are you okay?"

"Do you want to talk about it?"

"Would you like to come along?"

Write down 10 things you can ask or say to friends to show you care.

1. _____
2. _____
3. _____
4. _____
5. _____

6. _____
7. _____
8. _____
9. _____
10. _____

11. Problem-Solving

Sometimes I've noticed that my friends want to do something but things get in the way. What do you do when this happens to you?

Sarah wants to go to the movies with Cindy and me this weekend, but she doesn't have the money to go. What could she do?

_____

_____

_____

_____

_____

Ronald has asthma so he can't run as fast as everyone else. During gym class, he ends up running by himself, but feels stupid. What can he do?

_____

_____

_____

_____

Toby is really fun to be around, but he lives far away. I'd like to get to see him more often. What can I do?

_____

_____

_____

_____

_____

12. Recognizing Friendly Behaviors

Not everybody I know is good at being a friend, as this picture of my school yard at recess shows. Who in this picture is acting like a friend? Color in the friendly people who stand out.

13. Word Game

Hidden in this jumble of letters are six words that describe some things friends do together. Circle all the words you can find. (Hint: go up, down, sideways and diagonal.)

```
W E P L A Y D E
N Z S i A X M P
L O D S H U G V
E J U T R Q G S
C A R E A M B H
E X D N F L O C
R B S A J V K i
```

14. Your Garden of Feelings

When I have a good time with a person, I begin to have good, friendly feelings. Whenever I have another good time, the friendly feelings grow and grow. The flower shows how my friendship with Cindy has grown. Now think about your best friend. How did you meet? What happened next that made you want to be friends? What happened then? Write down what happened with your friend beside the flower. Then color it in.

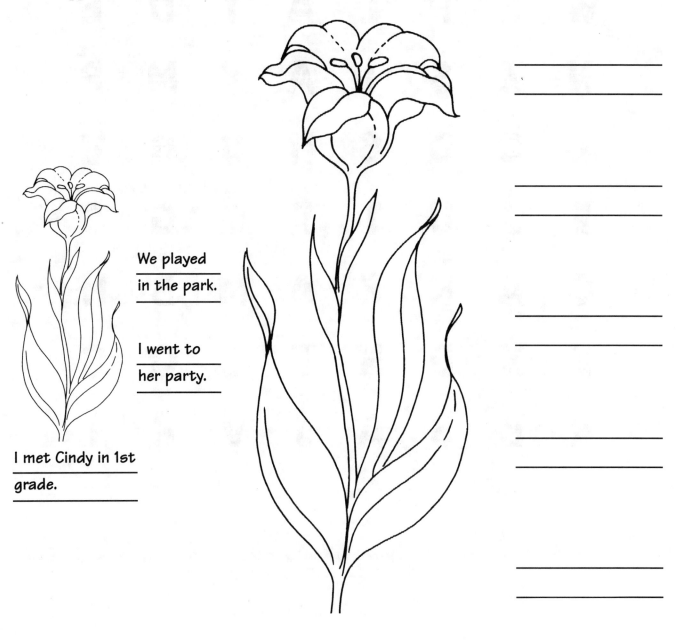

We played in the park.

I went to her party.

I met Cindy in 1st grade.

15. Your Secret Garden

Who would you like to have for a new friend? Write down the name of this secret friend. Write down when and how you met at the bottom of the picture. Then write down, at each leaf, some things you might do with this person in the future to help your friendship grow. Connect the dots to see how your friendship might flower.

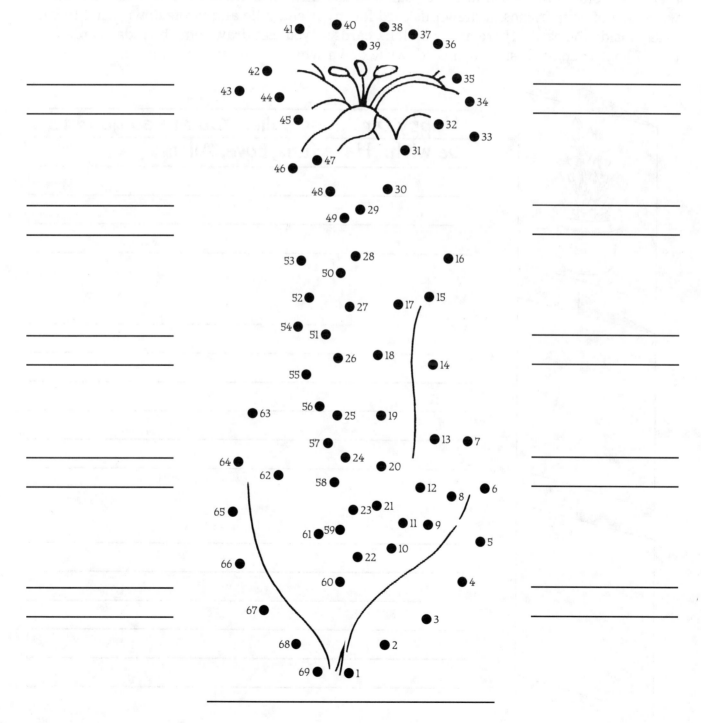

_____

_____

_____

_____

_____

_____

_____

_____

_____

_____

_____

_____

_____

_____

_____

_____

16. Friends' Birthdays Are Special

There is no one in the world just like me, and there is no one in the world just like you, and there is no one in the world just like your friends! Birthdays are a great time to celebrate with each of your friends. I drew this card for my friend Julie and wrote down what I want to say inside the card. There are two blank cards so you can draw some birthday cards for two of your friends. Beside each card, write down what you want to say inside.

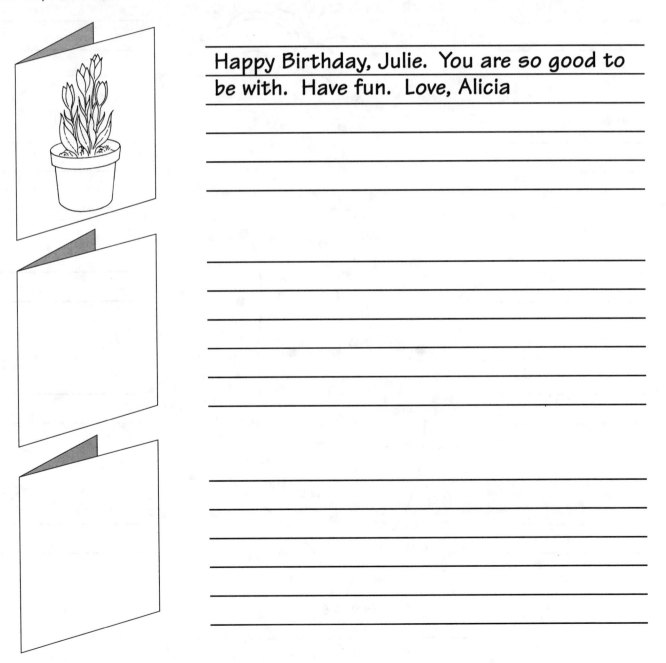

Happy Birthday, Julie. You are so good to be with. Have fun. Love, Alicia

17. The Giving Game (Part 1)

Giving presents can make everyone feel good. It feels good inside to think of something that my friend would really like, and then see her face when she opens the present. It makes me feel good about being friends and about myself. So I invented a game I call the "Giving Game." This is how you play:

Imagine that you could give your friends any present in the world. What would you give them? (I would give Sarah roller blades, because I know she really wants them.) Now you try it. Write down the names of your friends. In the picture frame beside their name, paste in a magazine picture of something that you would like to give to each one. If you can't find a picture, you can draw one in.

Sarah

18. The Giving Game (Part 2)

This is another way I play the Giving Game. I imagine that I want to give my friends a present, but it *can't cost anything*. It has to be something that I already have or that I can do for them. I can't really get Sarah roller blades, but I can teach her how to do the new dance that my brother Calvin taught me. This is something Sarah will be really happy to learn.

Now you try it. Write down the names of your friends. In the picture frame beside their name, paste in a magazine picture that shows something you can give to them or do for them or with them, for free. If you can't find a picture, you can draw one in, like this:

Sarah

_____   _____

_____   _____

19. Replay

Did you ever say anything you didn't mean to say? If you could talk to your friend all over again, what would you say differently? Write down what your friend said, what you said, and what you would say now.

My Friend Said:

i Said:

What i Would Say Now:

20. Red Light - Green Light

Talking to my mom about my problems makes me feel better. But sometimes, when something goes wrong with a friend, I don't always want to talk about it right away.

Think of something that went wrong with a friend. If you don't feel ready to talk about it yet, color in the red light on this traffic light. If you think you might be ready to talk about it, color in the yellow light. If you are sure you are ready to talk about it, color in the green light. Then go talk to someone who will listen and understand.

What Happened?

What Do You Want to Happen Now?

RED

YELLOW

GREEN

21. Letting Go

Sometimes things go wrong between friends. After a while, though, I want to forget about them and get back to being friends, no matter what. This activity helps me to do that:

Inside the dark clouds, I write down what went wrong. I color the cloud in with dark colors for all my sad feelings. Then I color in the bright sun and the wind chasing my dark cloud away. Now you try it.

22. Starting Over

Friends have good times *and* bad times, and still they stay friends.

Some of the pictures below show ways that friends can get back together. Some show pictures of ways that don't help. Think about these pictures. Cross out the ways that you think won't help people stay friends. Color in the ways that help people remain friends.

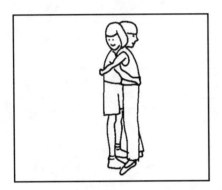  

23. Write a Letter

Write a letter to your best friend. Tell him/her how special he/she is. Write what you like best about him/her. If you like your letter, tear out this page or recopy your letter and give your letter to your friend. See what happens when you tell your friend how much you care.

Dear _____

_____

_____

_____

_____

_____

_____

_____

_____

_____

_____

_____

_____

Your friend, _____

24. Circle of Friends

The better I get at making friends, the more friends I have. I am getting so good at making friends, I think I am surrounded by them! As you get better at making friends, you will feel surrounded by them, too.

Draw your face on the figure in the center of the circle (or paste a photograph of your face if you are allowed to cut one out). Write your name under your picture. As you make friends, draw their faces on the figures around you and write their names underneath. Soon you will have a whole circle of friends you care about who care about you.

25. Making New Friends

All through life you will meet new people and have the chance to make new friends. But what are good ways to make new friends? Johnny just arrived from another country and started school at Maple Elementary.

These five children are each saying something that will make Johnny feel better about his first day of school. Can you think about what each one might be saying? Fill in the balloons in this picture.

26. Remembering Friends When They Move

When someone moves away, it doesn't mean that they can't still be your friend. Bobby moved away from his best friend David. Below are five pictures showing what happened when David left, but they are in the wrong order. Can you number them from 1 to 5 so that they show how Bobby and David said good-bye so that they would still be friends?

Number: _____

Number: _____

Number: _____

Number: _____

Number: _____

27. When You Lose a Friend

Have you ever had a friend, who suddenly stops being your friend? People act different ways when someone doesn't want to be their friend anymore. Draw a picture of someone who used to be your friend. Can you remember why your friendship ended?

28. When Friends Fight

Almost every friendship has some bad times. Even people who like each other very much will sometimes fight. Why do you think each of these friends had a fight? Write the reason underneath.

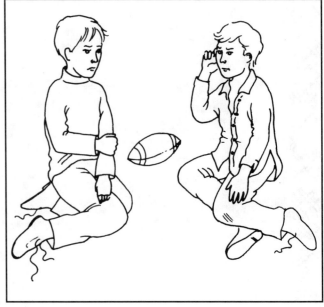

29. Choosing Between Friends

Have you ever had to choose between two friends that didn't like each other? That can be really hard to do. Can you think of three things that this girl could do to get her two friends to like each other?

1. _____

2. _____

3. _____

30. Keeping Friends

This is Barry. He has more friends than anyone I know. Can you see why? The word that best describes Barry is hidden in the picture with his friends. It is a four letter word beginning with "k."